DOING
GOOD

DOING GOOD

A Grace-Filled
Approach to Holiness

Christopher P.
Momany

Abingdon Press
Nashville

DOING GOOD
A GRACE-FILLED APPROACH TO HOLINESS
by Christopher P. Momany

Copyright © 2011

All rights reserved.

This book is printed on acid-free paper.

Library of Congress Cataloging-in-Publication Data

Momany, Christopher P.

Doing Good / Christopher P. Momany

p. cm.

ISBN 978-1-4267-0938-8 (alk. paper)

1. Christian life--Methodist authors. 2. Holiness. 3. Perfection--Religious aspects--Christianity. I. Title.

BV4501.3.M6465 2011

248.4'87--dc22

2010048799

ISBN-13: 978-1-426-70938-8

11 12 13 14 15 16 17 18 19 20—10 09 08 07 06 05 04 03 02 01

MANUFACTURED IN THE UNITED STATES OF AMERICA

Contents

Introduction

What is Christian holiness? This book attempts an answer to that question. For many, holiness is a kind of goodness they can never reach. For others, it is a religious doctrine once taught and now forgotten. For most, it is perhaps an intimidating or even irrelevant notion.

A story from my family history speaks clearly to confusion around the meaning of holiness. Late in the nineteenth century, people from the various Wesleyan denominations struggled to clarify the teaching of holiness. Many believed that the large, mainline Methodist bodies had already forgotten this emphasis of John Wesley. Some broke away to form churches that stressed a renewal of holiness.

My great-great Aunt Ella and Uncle Will were lifelong members of The Methodist Episcopal Church (a predecessor of The United Methodist Church), but one Sunday they were invited by a friend to attend the local "holiness" congregation. Wanting to demonstrate appropriate respect, they dressed in their best clothes. Aunt Ella wore a small watch attached to a gold chain, a gift that had been given to her by Uncle Will.

When they arrived at the church, they found themselves on the business end of a sermon that condemned fine clothes and jewelry. Evidently holiness meant not wearing the wrong thing. Aunt Ella and Uncle Will sat there calmly and took the heat without complaint, but the husband of the woman who invited them was outraged. He was not a regular church participant and had always been suspect in the eyes of his wife's congregation, but he knew the difference between kindness and rudeness. Why would you invite someone to church and then embarrass them in the name of holiness?

The next Sunday, this man appeared in church wearing his finest clothes and a huge log chain around his neck, attached to an alarm clock. He complicated his critique, though, by showing up quite drunk. The whole town almost fell apart over the controversy.

So is Christian holiness a matter of keeping petty rules; or is it knowing the difference between kindness and rudeness, even if one engages in questionable or wrong behavior? I suggest that holiness is neither of these two options. It is something else entirely. Holiness is living in relationship with God, not using minor rules against others. However, holiness is not living without regard for God's law or intended way of life for us.

The emphasis on holiness is a teaching peculiar to Wesleyan people. It is not a teaching exclusive to Wesleyan people. The notion of holiness has been around much longer than the followers of John Wesley, and it has been a concern of several different religious traditions. Yet there was a unique sensitivity to holiness among early Wesleyans, and I believe that this holiness witness is something of a neglected treasure waiting for rediscovery.

Two quandaries have tended to dominate discussions of Christian holiness. The first has dealt with a definition of the matter. The second has confronted the degree to which people can become holy. While many writers since John Wesley have sought to define the meaning of holiness, most have spent the bulk of their time considering whether living this way is possible. Over two hundred years of Wesleyan-related debate has raged regarding the viability of living a holy life. The discussion has not been made any easier by the terminology used in these disputes.

Most often holiness is associated with the curious language of Christian "perfection." This is not invented jargon. The Bible speaks of becoming perfect, perhaps most notably in Matthew 5:48. Yet again, what does this mean?

The discipline of theology has traditionally made a distinction between two great works of God in the life of believers. The first is linked to the forgiveness Christ offers. This is called justification. We are considered to be just as a gift from God in Christ, even though we do not merit such treatment. The second is linked to the growth in grace that takes place following justification. This is called sanctification. We are invited to become that which God has considered us to be. Holiness or Christian perfection is closely connected to sanctification. Holiness is the reality of becoming/being that which God desires for us.

However, even this description of holiness does not tell the entire story. If we conceive of holiness or Christian perfection or sanctification as a "process," we open ourselves to further questions. Can anyone ever reach it? Does it ever come all at once? How would we know if someone actually became all that God intended for that person? Perhaps we can understand why past dialogue regarding holiness has tended to move rather quickly from definitions to consideration of its possibility.

Many within the Wesleyan movement have expressed a conviction that holiness is a life-long journey. According to this perspective, we should not worry about identifying it so precisely. Others caution that such a process-oriented view amounts to neglecting the importance of holiness or explaining away its possibility in this life. Likewise, many understand holiness as a separation from the world, a cleansing from sin, and the refraining from certain behaviors. Others have understood it as engagement with the world for justice. The varied approaches can be perplexing, and they sometimes represent competing wings of the Wesleyan family.

However, most within the movement would affirm that holiness is nothing without love. Therefore a careful consideration of love confronts every seeker after holiness, and this consideration must be grounded in the biblical witness and informed by principled theological reflection.

We can appreciate the creative tension between process and event, between personal cleansing and social engagement; but we will not be dominated by these well-worn contrasts in this book. Instead we will explore the meaning of love as it speaks to our relationship with God and our relationships with others.

This approach does not promise a transparent resolution to past misunderstandings. In fact, the consideration of love opens a huge number of unresolved issues. Yet love is not a bad place to begin and end such reflection, and it may be the absolutely best place.

Here we will embrace the idea of holiness by examining such questions as its relationship to the moral law; its relationship to freedom; and, most importantly, its relationship to the very being of God. We will find that holiness is all about relationships—not smothering, controlling relationships, but one's essential relationship with God in Christ that leads to love for others.

Chapter One provides a context for the study. Christian holiness means different things to different people. Clarity and depth are only possible when the doctrine's history is explored. We will look at the meaning of holiness expressed in the Old and New Testaments, and we will take a brief look at the way this emphasis developed throughout Christianity. The central part of this chapter will revisit John Wesley's interpretation of holiness and how that tradition may point a way forward.

Chapter Two begins a series of movements. This chapter functions as a triad with Chapter Three and Chapter Four. Some might even suggest that the themes probed in Chapters Two, Three, and Four describe stages of Christian growth. It is tempting to consider the book from this vantage point;

but I hesitate to suggest that the movement from Chapter Two through Chapter Three and toward Chapter Four represents an orderly progression for spiritual life. Rather, the reader is invited to consider her or his life against the backdrop of the three chapters.

Chapter Two explores the importance of God's law in the life of holiness. Christians who value holiness inevitably note its connection with the moral law. They remind the church that grace is not a matter of neglecting the Law, and this message is critical. Yet sometimes holiness advocates have neglected grace in the pursuit of God's law. This flaw is not simply a theoretical oversight; it is often a cultural mindset that turns holiness into rule-keeping. Such a worldview can feed domineering attitudes where people control others through expectations that have little to do with the gospel.

Chapter Three explores the importance of grace and Christian freedom. Many (within and outside the church) know when something pretending to be the gospel is anything but good news. Yet real grace remains a mysterious reality.

The modern appreciation for freedom and autonomy reflects a partial truth. Religious demands can become burdens and even psychological weapons. Freedom from judgment and petty obligations feels like grace and may very well be an expression of grace. However, mere release from rules, regulations, and expectations is not necessarily a gift from God. Such "freedom" often becomes an independence that leads to isolation and even self-absorption.

Chapter Four moves beyond the shattering of human control and toward an embrace of relationship with God and others. Because this affirmation of relationships includes giving our lives away, it is a commitment. Yet it is not something we achieve. These relationships are created and sustained by grace.

It is a gift to be reconciled with God and others. Such a gift is not always fun, and it may not lead to our culture's idea of happiness. Still, the gift promises profound meaning through the most painful suffering and the most exhilarating joy. This embrace of relationship is what John Wesley described when he spoke about Christian perfection or holiness. Why not ponder holiness today as a blessing for our lives and for others?

CHAPTER ONE

Being Who We Are

"Be perfect, therefore, as your heavenly Father is perfect."

—Matthew 5:48

L ate in life, John Wesley wrote about the place of Christian perfection, or holiness, in the Methodist movement: "This doctrine is the grand depositum which God has lodged with the people called Methodists; and for the sake of propagating this chiefly he appeared to have raised us up."1 This quote has become something of a sound bite in Wesleyan lore. Yet it serves as a legitimately haunting reminder. The statement is more than simply an affirmation of holiness. It is a claim that the teaching of holiness was this movement's signature vocation.

Matters of vocation possess primal force. They capture the questions that dominate our lives and give them perspective. Purpose, mission, motivation, and direction are all taken up in vocation, a word that describes the experience of hearing God's voice. It is one thing for individuals to probe the meaning of vocation. It is something else entirely for a movement to own a singular vocation. Think of the possibilities: a renewal of vocational identity across the Wesleyan movement!

Holiness as an Old Testament Concept

Conceptions of holiness have been around for ages. The Old Testament Hebrew typically employs some form of the term *qadhosh* when speaking of holiness, and different parts of the Old Testament emphasize different aspects of the word. We should remember that holiness begins with the identity of God. God is holy, but what does that mean?

Generally speaking, Hebrew traditions considered holiness a state of being set apart or consecrated for particular service. The Book of Leviticus gives us the most comprehensive picture of holiness among the Old Testament world. Inanimate objects could be holy (Leviticus 8:10-11), but so could people (Leviticus 8:12). The uniqueness associated with holiness implied a separation from the ordinary. The fundamental distinction between God and the natural world grounded all conceptions of holiness.

If God was the very standard of holiness, then only that related to God could approximate this quality. There is much in the Old Testament that conceives of holiness as a relational reality, an attribute received from association with God. After all, consecration entails a devotion to some being or purpose outside of the self. However, the proximity with God was matched by a distancing from other earthly things. The holy was, by implication, separated from the common.

This separation was perhaps most explicit in the ritual and dietary practices of holiness. Such traditions set God's people apart from surrounding culture. Contemporary readers might find it easy to dismiss the layers of dietary minutia and ritual detail, but these instructions served to celebrate closeness with God as much as they differentiated the faithful.

Leviticus 17–26 is often called the Holiness Code, and Leviticus 19 makes explicit that holiness is a response to God: "You shall be holy, for I the LORD your God am holy" (Leviticus 19:2). This chapter contains plenty of concern for ritual, but it also displays a commitment to justice. The ritual and the moral are intimately related in most Old Testament conceptions of holiness. Those commanded to keep the sabbath and shun idols were also to care for the poor and for strangers (Leviticus 19:9-10). Stealing was condemned, and honesty was expected (Leviticus 19:11-13). In fact, the call to neighbor love is notably expressed here (Leviticus 19:18).

We should be careful about concluding that Old Testament conceptions of holiness were one-dimensional and obsessed with purity for its own sake. Purity was another way of indicating dedication to God, and dedication to God certainly made people unique. There are several examples of exclusionary behavior in the Old Testament, even as there are cliques in today's church. Yet at its best, holiness entailed a compassionate awareness of others. If holiness involves a consecration to some higher purpose, then Wesleyans might consider their special calling given by God on behalf of the world.

Holiness as a New Testament Concept

New Testament approaches to holiness most often relate to the Greek word *hagios*. The various types of New Testament literature all display particular emphases; but they also share a basic conviction: Holiness is given ultimate definition through the life, death, and resurrection of Jesus. Moreover, the notion of holiness is closely identified with the meaning of sanctification. New Testament understandings of holiness and sanctification extend the paradox of being set apart and offered up for others.

The connection between holiness and sacrifice is exceedingly prominent in Hebrews. Here the work of God is described as a hallowed mission to redeem creation through Jesus' self-giving love (Hebrews 9:23-28). The ritualistic aspects of Old Testament holiness are evident in this document, but the stress remains on the once and conclusive act of God in Christ (10:1-18). Thus a profound aspect of God's holiness is revealed in the willingness to enter the world, suffer, and overcome sin on behalf of all people.

Likewise, Paul stressed the work of God in Christ. Over the years, Paul's letters have been at the center of debate regarding the possibility or impossibility of reaching entire sanctification during this life. Yet the extraordinary initiative of God through Jesus occupied the apostle's primary energy. Holiness was God's business before it became a matter of theological controversy. This is especially apparent in Philippians 2, though it is woven throughout the body of Paul's writing. Therefore the contours of holiness found in the Gospels must be understood in light of all that God accomplished through Christ, and the holiness available to followers of Christ embodies costly love and ultimate triumph.

The primacy of God's redeeming love situates everything Jesus commanded that might be described as holiness. The Sermon on the Mount (Matthew 5–7) is a classic example. Many have read these chapters as instruction requiring moral achievement; however, they are visions of the life available to believers given God's great redemption. The language of Matthew 5:48 is particularly jarring: "Be perfect, therefore, as your heavenly Father is perfect." Could there be a more intimidating command?

However, even this instruction regarding perfection is a call to enter the reality unveiled when Jesus went to the cross and rose from the grave for all people. Matthew 5–7 is not a code or series of rules. It is a world of possibility.

The terminology of perfection is derived from the Greek word *teleios*. The meaning suggests holiness or sanctification and implies maturation, wholeness as a person, reaching God's intended purpose. On its own the word is as daunting as any command in Matthew 5–7, and our contemporary culture is awash with sick and twisted conceptions of "perfection." Yet a perfection that blooms in the light of God's sacrificial love is something else entirely. This is a perfection or wholeness that knows the marvelously liberating truth: The holy God climbed down into history and gave his life so that we might live. Why not step into that promise?

The Journey of John Wesley

John Wesley's relentless pursuit of Christian perfection, or holiness, therefore continued a rich and lively tradition. Wesley described the founding of Methodism as a quest for holiness that began in 1725. This does not mean that he ended his days with the same understanding of holiness possessed while a young man. It simply means that in spite of growth and change, the life of holiness remained consistently on Wesley's personal horizon; and all that time he acknowledged that this was an inherited vision. Wesley was especially influenced by his reading of William Law's book *A Serious Call to a Devout and Holy Life* (1729).

The earnestness of John Wesley's desire for holiness led him to the American colonies, where he dreamed of a successful missionary enterprise. Instead, he encountered something many holiness hopefuls confront at one time or another: failure. A less-than-impressive ministry, a botched romance, a misunderstanding, and broken relationships all drove him back to England. If holiness was an achievement, then Wesley's life did not meet the measure.

Such was the run-up to John Wesley's well-documented Aldersgate experience of May 24, 1738. While attending an evening meeting, Wesley's heart was warmed by the good news. The downcast holiness seeker bumped up against the grace of God in Christ. Scholars debate the significance of this conversion-like event. One can argue that Wesley did not understand the gift of salvation at all before 1738, or one might argue that he gained a new appreciation for the role of grace in sanctification. Regardless, the Wesleyan legacy came to rest on grace. Growth is not accomplished by dint of will. It is a gift, even as forgiveness itself is a gift.

The remainder of Wesley's ministry included a series of explanations regarding his approach to holiness or sanctification, and he boldly embraced the language of perfection. In his 1741 sermon "Christian Perfection," Wesley set out to clarify and defend his perspective. He claimed that perfection "is only another term for holiness. They are two names for the same thing."[2] Yet he realized that many would object to his views. Definitions were therefore critical.

Wesley proposed to describe ways that mature Christians are not perfect and ways that they might be considered perfect. First, Christians cannot be perfectly free from ignorance. Knowledge is limited to time and place. The most mature follower of Christ will find that he or she labors under finite understanding.

Second, Christians cannot be perfectly free from mistakes. Given limitations of awareness or knowledge, unintended errors are bound to be made. Third, Christians cannot be perfectly free from "infirmities." Wesley's choice of word here is unusual, and he meant something particular. Sin is not an infirmity. The term describes those unsolicited conditions of body or mind that challenge us.

Finally, Christians cannot be perfectly free from temptation. Even the most mature people of faith face subtle or not-so-subtle enticement to do wrong. Holy people draw upon the resources of God to resist temptation.

Wesley then made an attempt to describe ways that mature Christians might be considered perfect. This part of the teaching is less clear and tends to sound like typical arguments regarding the possibility or impossibility of reaching perfection. Yet there is a profound movement near the end of Wesley's sermon that invites sustained reflection. He likens holiness to living the language found in Galatians 2:19-20: "I have been crucified with Christ; and it is no longer I who live, but it is Christ who lives in me. And the life I now live in the flesh I live by faith in the Son of God who loved me and gave himself for me."

Holiness entails death to one's self and the resurrection to a new self. The old self seeks to establish itself before God through effort, excellence, competence, and achievement. The new self can only be conceived in relationship with Christ. This resurrected self completes personhood. Christ does not annihilate identity but creates new identity for believers. On the one hand, an individual separated from God can never measure up. On the other hand, a constant relationship with Christ does not neglect moral standards. Rather, the new self is defined by love; and love is a matter of relationship with God and others.

This emphasis on love grounded Wesley's most comprehensive treatment of holiness. His essay "A Plain Account of Christian Perfection" bundled up key convictions, objections, and clarifications regarding the holiness teaching of early Methodists. Overall, Wesley considered love a matter of pure intention. His reading of Scripture appreciated the critical nature of one's inner life. What motivates us? Why do we act as we do? Are we fixed on God and our neighbors? These questions are important, but the concern for intention can miss some things. What about those times when we hurt others, even though our intent seems pure?

Wesley's theology might allow one to consider such harm a mistake due to unavoidable limitations, but can we be sure? Are our intentions always as pristine as we claim; and if someone is hurt in the end, do good intentions matter? The world is populated by Christians who profess pure hearts but neglect or disrespect others. Let's come clean. Wesley's notion of holiness as love can be manipulated to emphasize the acting subject while disregarding the object or results of behavior.

This caution does not mean that those who appreciate holiness today should only stress outcomes or consequences. The obsession with results is as dangerous as any exclusive concern for intention. We are, nonetheless, challenged to think deeper about the character of love. How we do this may make a contribution to the holiness witness.

Holiness After Wesley

Followers of John Wesley were captivated and baffled by his devotion to holiness. American Methodism embraced the tradition, but some thought the doctrine had been neglected by the Civil War. A variety of writers, pastors, and seekers after God revisited the teaching. Some dismissed it; others affirmed its possibility. Some thought it to be an instantaneously available gift from God; others stressed holiness as a gradual process. Still others gave the teaching a whole new orientation.

During the early and middle nineteenth century, questions about Christian perfection or holiness spread well beyond established Methodist circles. Catholic writers had long kept the emphasis alive, but other Protestant traditions also entered the conversation. Those who affirmed some form of holiness teaching often coupled its moral message with social reform. The antislavery and women's rights movements of the early 1800's were indebted to Christian holiness advocates.

One particularly powerful combination of holiness teaching and social reform blossomed at Oberlin College in Ohio after 1835. That year a young pastor named Asa Mahan became president of the struggling college; and Charles Finney, a noted evangelist, joined the faculty as professor of theology. Mahan and Finney studied and then embraced the doctrine of Christian perfection.

Not surprisingly, the Oberlin movement owed much to John Wesley, even though the president and chief professor came from Presbyterian backgrounds. In 1839, Mahan wrote a provocative book called *Scripture Doctrine of Christian Perfection*. Mahan defined Christian perfection in a manner that echoed Wesley: "It is 'loving the Lord our God with all our heart, and with all our soul, and with all our strength, and our neighbor as ourselves.' It implies the entire absence of all selfishness, and the perpetual presence and all pervading influence of pure and perfect love."[3] Yet once again, we are left with the question, What is authentic love?

Mahan was not simply a preacher and teacher of holiness. He was also an able philosopher, and he applied his philosophical precision to a definition of *love*. Mahan invoked the scriptural statement that love fulfills the moral law (Romans 13:10), and he claimed that there are basically two options for determining this law. First, one might discern obligation by calculating the end one wishes to achieve. Second, one might discern right and wrong by considering the value of those who receive our actions. Mahan was committed to the second principle.

This focus on the value of others allowed Mahan to teach that holiness was love but that love was more than only good intentions or the creation of outcomes. Love, for Mahan, required treating others according to their intrinsic worth; and intrinsic worth was understood to be one's value regardless of faults or "usefulness." Theologically speaking, this worth is established by God through creation and redemption. Scripture teaches that all people are created in the image of God. Some might qualify the lasting impact of this dignity, due to sin; but the gospel teaches that, even so, people are granted restored value through the cross and the Resurrection.

Love Defined by the Cross

It is commonplace to consider the cross God's ultimate expression of sacrificial love. There is good reason for such an understanding. The cross is the intersection of awe-inspiring dynamics. The holy God entered history and gave of the self, unto death, that we might live. The cross and its mysteries also invite endless speculation regarding the meaning of atonement, the gift of reconciliation with God.

Some stress the guilt of humanity and the wrath of God that could only be satisfied on the cross. Others, especially in the modern age, have avoided the sacrificial themes of the cross. For them the Crucifixion has been explained by a harsh theology. However, we need not dwell on human calculations of desert and punishment to wonder at the gift of love demonstrated on the cross. Likewise, we dare not turn away from the cross because it offends some modern presumption. The cross is an absolutely critical determiner of love.

If holiness has traditionally been defined by separation, then the cross of Jesus illustrates the great paradox of love. Only the holy God could save, and the holy God saved by participating in humanity. When those representing the power of political, ethnic, class, and social separation were offended by the life of Jesus, they made sure that he ended up dead. Through his death, God expressed ultimate identification with human experience. The refusal to stop loving was a dangerous act, and the consequences of this freely chosen resistance magnified God's love.

Wesleyans hold that the sacrificial death of Jesus remains a gift for all people. This is not to say that all will receive the gift of new relationship. Yet the offer stands. There are Christian traditions that do not believe Jesus died for all. They hold a doctrine of "election." The sacrifice expressed by Jesus is considered an act on behalf of those destined for heaven. Wesleyans believe that this restrictive understanding of the cross amounts to a limitation on God's love. It can also open exclusionary assumptions regarding people. What about the value of those who are not considered the recipients of God's sacrificial love?

If the cross of Jesus embodies God's love, it also fixes the worth of humanity. God was not obligated to demonstrate extreme sacrifice. God's love created and recreated intrinsic worth. This value applies to all, even those who struggle to receive the truth. Wesleyans agree that we love others because God loves us. Yet the others we love are not questionable beneficiaries of our high-minded generosity. They are people loved by God—people given ultimate value by God's amazing gift on the cross.

Love Defined by the Resurrection

The power of sacrificial death is so strong that we might miss the connection between Jesus' resurrection and God's love. Easter is a triumph, but it is not a triumph made for our culture's obsession with winning. In fact, the Resurrection is such an unlikely reality that it still meets much skepticism. Christians may feel a sense of vindication in the Easter story, but the ongoing meaning of the event does not encourage self-importance. There is as much paradox in the Resurrection as there is in the cross.

On the one hand, the resurrection of Jesus points to the lordship of God in Christ. Conventional categories of the natural world do not rule. God reigns. On the other hand, the risen Lord dwells in times and places that are not customarily associated with power. Matthew 25:31-46 (the judgment of the nations) illustrates the dynamic well. This text is understandably linked to the idea of final accountability, but the judgment is also associated with the presence of God.

Those ushered into the kingdom are those who loved the Lord: "And the king will answer them, 'Truly I tell you, just as you did it to one of the least of these who are members of my family, you did it to me'" (Matthew 25:40). Many read this as a command to love powerless people, and it certainly bears such implications. Yet often readers of the text conclude that when we love the powerless, it is "as if" we love Jesus. Why not read the text as written? When we love the forgotten, we *do* love Jesus. The risen Jesus chooses to dwell, or live, with those overlooked by the world. If worth is given for all through the sacrificial death on the cross, then it is also given by the ongoing presence of God.

Asa Mahan had it right. The objective value of others, even those outside the power structures of society, measures our love. The fact that Jesus died for us provides plenty of motivation. We love as a matter of gratitude, and there is nothing wrong with good intent. Likewise, the desire to create good outcomes has a place in our actions. However, love is much more than our intentions and agendas. It is getting over the self long enough to affirm those loved on the cross and those who host the risen Lord.

Some years ago I received a moving gift. Not long before, my brother married a woman from the Amana Colonies in Iowa; and our family came to know and love this community. Amana is a cluster of small towns and the home of a devout Christian body that traces its origins to German Protestantism. Members of the Amana Church love visitors, but they also have a tight-knit sense of identity. They are rightfully proud of their history, and it is a unique heritage. Many of the members still speak German, unless in the company of guests. Amana is known for many fine crafts: furniture, clocks, woolens, and quilts. An Amana quilt is something to treasure.

When I graduated college, a group of women from the colonies gave me a specially designed, handmade quilt. The quilt was unmistakably Amana in its quality and character, but it also featured the United Methodist cross and flame. Those who labored over the gift knew that I was planning to become a pastor. For years I have pondered the symbolism of that gesture. A group of women, particular and comfortable with their identity, chose to affirm my identity and call. They graced me. We need a revitalized holiness heritage like that—unafraid to be unique while at the same time bold enough to affirm others.

---

1. From *The Works of John Wesley*, Volume XIII (Baker Book House, 1986); page 9.
2. From *The Works of John Wesley*, Volume 2, edited by Albert C. Outler (Abingdon Press, 1985); page 104.
3. From *Scripture Doctrine of Christian Perfection*, by Asa Mahan (D. S. King, 1839); page 10.

CHAPTER TWO

Beyond Do's and Don'ts

*"For by grace you have been saved through faith, and
this is not your own doing; it is the gift of God."*
—*Ephesians 2:8*

When a friend of mine attended seminary, he discovered an intriguing policy at his theological school. In an attempt to honor the sabbath commandment, the institution's gymnasium and exercise facility were closed on Sunday. However, the library was not. Every Sunday afternoon and evening the theological library buzzed with activity.

I love libraries. I love their collections and their role in learning. They are repositories of discovery and resources for intellectual growth. Yet the library at a graduate theological school is also a place of toil—a research environment for those writing papers, studying for exams, or simply keeping up with course expectations.

The sabbath commandment is an example of God's law offering grace. Once a week, we receive the gift of rest; and life continues. Our value does not come from performance; and when we stop for a while, we can internalize this wonderful news. Isn't it odd that physical exercise was suspended but striving to prove the self was not? God's law is good, but our manipulation of it is a problem. Time and again the gracious authority of God's law is co-opted by humans and made a burden.

Oppressive Law, No Law, and Good News

An insightful part of Asa Mahan's *Christian Perfection* addresses the way God's law relates to the life of holiness. Mahan suggested that there are three ways to view God's law. The first is legalism. This approach attempts to earn God's favor through effort. The second is antinomianism. This technical (and perhaps unfamiliar) term contains the Greek word *nomos*, meaning "law." Essentially, antinomianism is a disregard for the law. It is a view that some fall into when they claim that grace makes God's law unimportant.

However, Mahan believed that beyond these two approaches there was a third, life-giving truth. This he called the evangelical spirit. Mahan spoke of something specific when he used such language. The word *evangelical* comes from the Greek, meaning "good news." Mahan was not referring to a modern-day religious movement or ideological party. He employed the term to celebrate good news beyond the despair of legalism and antinomianism.

Just what is this good news? It is grace—God's gift of the self. Legalism and antinomianism are opposite sides of the same coin. They leave us to our own devices. The good news breaks through when we realize that we are not alone. We do not have to keep the Law by revving up our will power. We do not have to invent excuses for why we fail. We can receive the gift of a relationship with God through Jesus Christ; and God's law has always been—first and last—about this relationship and about relationships with others.

The Law of God in Biblical Perspective

The Old Testament includes several terms that aim to describe the Law, but the most comprehensive word is *torah*. The Hebrew language suggests teaching. *Torah* is not abstract legal expectation but inherited communication that serves a purpose.

People often begin reflection on God's law by looking to the Ten Commandments. This is understandable. The biblical witness expresses varied approaches to the meaning of law, but it would be something other than itself without the story of Moses on Mount Sinai. The law of God did not originate with these commandments. However, they serve as the root of subsequent obligations. Scholars have identified points of similarity between the Torah and surrounding ancient Near Eastern traditions, but similarity is not equivalence. The law of God grounded everything unique about the Hebrew people, and the community's most distinctive quality was its relationship with God.

A little reflection demonstrates that the Ten Commandments themselves point to this relationship. They begin: "I am the LORD your God, who brought you out of the land of Egypt, out of the house of slavery" (Exodus 20:2). Not only did the relationship between God and the people paint a backdrop for the commandments, the relationship was established by grace. God bent low to redeem the people. This is the God who called for adherence to a certain way of life.

The Old Testament is littered with the folly of broken relationships, especially the one between God and the people; but this does not mean that the Law was a bust. Rather, deceitful hearts misconstrued and misused the Law. That is one reason why Jeremiah 31 has invited such attention over the years. Here God promised to write the Law on the hearts of people. Coming at a time when Israel faced military disaster and moral failure, this promise meant something.

The new heart would shape one's core identity, and Jeremiah passed along the divine purpose of such change: "I will be their God, and they shall be my people" (Jeremiah 31:33). The following verse spells out the character of this intimacy. The people would no longer *know about* God; they would *know* God. The Law was a blessing and a way to remain close with God.

Some presume that the New Testament entails a rejection of the Torah, but the matter is more profound. Jesus did not discard the Law, but human attempts to manipulate the Law were judged and found wanting. The four Gospels present a diverse engagement of Jesus with the Law, but perhaps most notable is the statement in Matthew 5:17: " 'Do not think that I have come to abolish the law or the prophets; I have come not to abolish but to fulfill.' " The life, death, and resurrection of Jesus are good news precisely because they arrive as initiatives from God. We need not work our way to God. God acted first. Our lives can be a response to this gift, and such response can demonstrate the Law's goodness.

Even the apostle Paul says as much. The Letter to the Romans stands as his masterwork regarding salvation by grace through faith. Yet this very document includes the affirmation: "So the law is holy, and the commandment is holy and just and good" (Romans 7:12). Paul certainly probed the complicated rapport between law and grace, but his underlying message stressed the futility of (and lack of need for) attempts to manipulate the Law. The Law is not a tool for achievement; and whenever treated as such, it becomes something other than the law God designed.

Perhaps this is why Paul could also say, "Love does no wrong to a neighbor; therefore, love is the fulfilling of the law" (Romans 13:10). This love is not an endeavor to earn merit or a means to make claims upon God. It is the giving of self to others. It is the offer of relationship by those who know a giving God.

Law in the Wesleyan Tradition

The juxtaposition of law and grace shaped much of Christian history. By the sixteenth century, many felt that the church's elaborate system of canon law invited corruption. The events leading to Martin Luther's movement exposed a neglect of grace and an exploitation of the Law for personal and collective gain. If people were saved by following church rules, then opportunity existed for an abuse of power. Luther's insistence that salvation arrived by grace through faith short-circuited the apparatus of church control and pointed toward God's prerogative. It also disrupted certain understandings of the Law.

What, after all, was the proper role of God's law in the Christian life? Martin Luther did not repudiate the Law. Rather, he gave it careful respect within the dynamics of salvation. Put simply, Luther believed there were two "uses" of the Law. The first was a civil use that restrained bad behavior and protected the innocent. The second was a theological use that confronted people with their shortcomings and sin. This second use of the Law drove people to Christ and the gift of grace. Nowhere in Luther's view was the Law a vehicle for earning salvation.

The Lutheran perspective came to be the gold standard for Protestant conceptions of the Law. However, it was modified significantly by later writers, especially John Calvin and his followers. Calvin accepted a third use of the Law. This scrupulously considered purpose of the Law emphasized a positive function. The Law might inspire those saved by grace to lead more honorable lives. The Law could not save, but perhaps it could guide.

John Wesley inherited the varied contours of these Protestant views. We might conclude that his early life of earnest striving amounted to legalism, a bondage that found relief during the Aldersgate experience. Yet the remainder of Wesley's life required a subtle appreciation for God's Law. If he celebrated his Aldersgate freedom without regard for the Law, then he risked antinomianism. If he continued his earlier obsession with the Law, then he risked a return to legalism. This dilemma was not only personal; it also confronted the growing Methodist movement. Several followers of Wesley traveled down the antinomian road once they grasped the miracle of grace, and he needed to counter this error. Others turned Wesley's message into a moralism that neglected grace, and he needed to correct this problem.

Perhaps Wesley's most articulate interpretation of God's law appeared in a series of three sermons. This treatment follows his thirteen sermons related to the Sermon on the Mount (Matthew 5–7). Wesley adopted a threefold appreciation for God's law that is reminiscent of Calvin. While John Wesley departed from Calvin in significant ways, he embraced the third use of God's law.

Wesley gave his views their own peculiar expression. He preferred to say that the Law (1) convinces sinners of their wrong, (2) converts people by leading them to Christ, and (3) sustains believers once they know grace. There may be little difference between Calvin's notion of the Law guiding and Wesley's insistence that it sustains, but one distinction remained. Wesley came to affirm that subsequent to salvation by grace, believers might actually live the Law that sustained or guided them.

Many have concluded that Wesley's bold conviction was overly optimistic, that it displayed an unsophisticated confidence in human ability to keep God's law. Yet this assessment focuses on the powers and failures of people. Wesley's audacious claim regarding the Law's third use says more about the Law than it does about people.

The law of God, for Wesley, was much more than a series of rules. It was much more than an elaborate philosophical code. It was much more than an impersonal standard of righteousness. Wesley understood the Law as a revelation of God's essence, God's innermost being. There was something intense and tender about John Wesley's conception of the Law.

At one point he described the Law as "a copy of the eternal mind, a transcript of the divine nature."[1] Through the Law, God did not simply issue orders and expectations. God offered the divine self. The Law, for Wesley, was a gift; and this gift was not external to God. The Law expressed

God's desire to embrace humanity. That is why Wesley also said that the Law "is the face of God unveiled."[2] The implications of such a statement are astounding.

Biblical language about God's face implies a splendor on the far horizon of human experience. Jacob wrestled with God and claimed to have met him face to face, but he also received a limp from the encounter (Genesis 32:30). Moses was known for his face-to-face relationship with God (Exodus 33:11), but an aspect of God's presence remained too searing for him (Exodus 33:20-23). John Wesley did not toss off casual theological statements. If he described the Law as an unveiling of God's face, he meant to describe something awesome. The evidence points to an insight that is at once simple and deep. Wesley believed that the Law represented an offer of intimate relationship.

Legalism and Social Control

From a human standpoint, there is perhaps only one problem with receiving a gift. Recipients cannot control the reality created by such giving. There are times, of course, when "gifts" offered by others are controlling; and it is wise to recognize those situations. Yet the receipt of God's gift is something else altogether. When we receive God's offer of self, we are not in control; and we also need not fear unhealthy control. In fact, receipt of this gift creates newness and life for us.

So how does God's law become something other than an authentic gift? This happens when we approach the Law as a means to earn favor with God or when humans seize it as a means to manipulate one another. The first scenario entails an assertion of the self that seeks to obligate God. The second scenario entails an assertion of the self in order to control others or the experience of controlling behavior by others. None of these cases involve the gift of relationship.

Society in general and the church are vexed by controlling relationships. On the one hand, human nature strives after worth, as if we can prove something to God. On the other hand, people often nurture petty expectations, rules, and judgments, as if we must prove something to one another. Both of these dynamics lack grace. Grace is unconditional. The legalism that typifies attempts to earn God's favor or the control between people is exceedingly conditional.

A conditional relationship is one founded on the connection between *if* and *then*. If one is a certain way, then one receives approval. The crudest forms of conditional acceptance are those that emphasize external traits: how people look, for instance. The abusive character of these attitudes is not hard to spot though not necessarily easy to end. More complicated are conditional relationships around behavior. If one acts a certain way, then one receives approval.

This second form of legalism requires deeper reflection. We need not agree with all behaviors to love others. Some behaviors are themselves abusive and based on the most controlling and conditional thinking. Yet we can find ways to affirm the being of others beyond behavior. Living this affirmation is often difficult for church people, and many unaffiliated with "organized religion" experience the church as an extremely conditional place.

Theologian Paul Tillich had a name for attempts to make God's law conditional. He called it "heteronomy."[3] The term comes from the Greek, meaning "outside or other" and "law." Heteronomy conceives of the Law as a device to be used against people. Those manipulated feel that the Law is outside of them and pointed at them, controlling them. It is a big stick that hangs over the head. Curiously, God's law also comes from beyond the self; but it cannot be wielded by other people. That is a critical distinction. Heteronomy is no gift.

When the Law is not shared as a gift, it becomes something ungodly. It becomes a weapon, and people unacquainted with the gospel are put off by attacks. It is that simple. All of the evangelistic techniques in the world cannot overcome judgmental hearts. There is a reason why we are still amazed with Jesus. He displayed the unconditional manner in which God receives people. This does not mean that Christians have perpetrated a two-thousand-year conspiracy against the good news, but sometimes it seems that way.

Only by sheer miracle has the gospel thrived in spite of personal and institutional manipulation. The fact that grace has survived our distortions and self-justifying assertions is one of its most compelling facets. People are starving for a God who is stronger than their crooked ways. They do not need us to remind them of failure, but we might remind them that this God of power and glory is also a God of love and affirmation.

Measuring Ourselves to Death

Legalism is a tricky beast. One might claim that it is the unique weakness of conservative religious bodies or at least those groups dominated by doctrinal rules and regulations. Some may feel better drawing this conclusion, but it does not pass the smell test. For every so-called conservative example of heteronomy, there is a corresponding expression of control among "liberal" people. Legalism is no respecter of ideology.

The mainline church is quite adept at misunderstanding God's law. One of the most exclusionary forces is the language we use, especially the acronyms for boards, agencies, and administrative organizations. In United Methodism, for example, we sometimes act as if it is more important to know the meaning of CCOM, BOM, and CFA than the Holy Trinity. Insider jargon and power plays around budgets are killing us.

I work in campus ministry at a United Methodist-related college. One blessing of such work is the relationships formed with students from a variety of traditions. Our United Methodist young people offer inspiring leadership, but there is a warm sense of equity and inclusion among the coordinated ministries. It is not helpful when denominational officials suggest that I focus on "our" students. Are they not *all* "our" people?

Likewise, I help lead a pre-seminary program that has experienced much growth in recent years. Young people are hearing God's call in amazing ways. Many of these students are already members of the denomination I represent, but others are not. Several of those from other traditions have grown through events and teaching sponsored by the mainline church. They actually think we are about the wonderfully good news of Christ crucified and resurrected. Some want to join our expression of the faith. I hope they will find us a generous and grace-empowered community.

Yet perhaps the most ominous threat of legalism in mainline Wesleyanism is our preoccupation with standards borrowed from the business world. As established denominations struggle against decline, many have embraced criteria from our economic culture to measure success and failure. There is probably something to be learned from specific business models, and many businesses practice biblical principles. However, the church was not founded as an economic exchange; and we had better think before wrapping our theology around notions that worship the bottom line.

Many of these imported management theories conceive of people as "customers," and customer-based strategies are inherently conditional. Customers receive services for a price. There is nothing wrong with this when it applies to legitimate business transactions, but it is hardly the logic of grace.

Church leaders enticed by such views do not intend to undermine the gospel. However, that danger comes with the territory. Conditional dynamics are not legalistic simply because they contain an if-and-then construction. They are also conditional because they measure everything (and often everyone) according to results. The relationship between means and ends is critical. Business models may not always claim that the end justifies the means, but they inevitably calculate worth according to the end desired. Even people can become a means to these ends.

Jesus never treated people as a means to an end. In God's economy people are ends in themselves. Why would we celebrate a system that uses people to accomplish the agendas of those with power? In an attempt to grow the church, some have neglected the truth our world is craving. People can find themselves used in a multitude of settings. Where can they find the unique affirmation of value offered by God in Christ?

It has been said that reticence about popular business models is simply an unwillingness to try new things. Others say that critique of these models amounts to fear and backward thinking. However, it seems to me that we have already been given the greatest news in human history—the gospel of grace! Why are we afraid to trust that, share that, and articulate the uniqueness of that amazing reality? New ways of proclaiming grace and affirmation are one thing. Why give ourselves to alien philosophies that are not inspired by the unconditional gift of God's love?

When law and gospel are received as divine gifts, they bring life. Techniques, programs, and marketing campaigns are merely ways to announce God's prerogative of grace. Imagine what might happen if our theology of redemption moved us to reflect carefully on the relationship between means and ends. We would discover that God's people are the end, and this realization is good news. Assessing ourselves by the world's standards is not only wrong. At the same time it misses an exciting opportunity to articulate grace.

Legalism may have superficial allure for a limited period, but it cannot sustain us. At best it is the worst kind of sliding scale that measures us against others. Wouldn't it be terrific to rest in an awareness of God's love and then live boldly for others? There is a better way than that of legalism, but to know this way we have to let go of some things.

We must let go of the need to justify ourselves and let go of the need to control others.

I am reminded of a critical time in the history of American Methodism. It was 1880, and a small number of women presented themselves to The Methodist Episcopal Church for ordination. One of these women was Anna Howard Shaw—brilliant, courageous, and well-credentialed with a graduate theological education. She was serving a church already and was admired by many people. Still, her denomination would not ordain her.

Shaw was at a loss regarding the future when a representative from The Methodist Protestant Church invited her to apply for ordination. Perhaps this church body would affirm her. She appeared before a conference held at Tarrytown, New York, in October 1880.

During a tense moment in the gathering, someone objected that Shaw was not yet a formal member of The Methodist Protestant Church. Why should the conference consider ordaining her? At that, the Reverend Lyman E. Davis, pastor of Beekman Avenue Methodist Protestant Church in the host city, called members of his congregation together. They quickly received Anna Howard Shaw into membership of the local congregation.

Davis returned to the conference meeting, as if to inquire whether there were any more objections! Unfortunately, there were; but soon the resistance to Shaw faded. The matter was settled, and she was ordained on October 12, 1880.[4]

Today we need witnesses like Anna Howard Shaw and Lyman Davis who will confront our controlling behavior when God has something powerful in mind. Such challenging actions are nothing less than expressions of grace.

1. From *The Works of John Wesley* (Outler); page 10.
2. From *The Works of John Wesley* (Outler); page 9.
3. From *Systematic Theology,* Volume 1, "Reason and Revelation Being and God," by Paul Tillich (The University of Chicago Press, 1951); pages 83-86.
4. From *The Story of a Pioneer,* by Anna Howard Shaw (Harper & Brothers Publishers, 1915); pages 122-30.

CHAPTER THREE

When Freedom Means Self-Absorption

"Do we then overthrow the law by this faith? By no means! On the contrary, we uphold the law."
—Romans 3:31

M any have known some version of my experience. I was working at my home computer, hustling to make a deadline, and the telephone rang. I answered, but no one was on the line. I hung up and returned to my work. Soon the phone rang again, and once more I answered. No one was on the line—again. By this time I was quite irritated and slammed the telephone down. Within five minutes the phone rang, and I cringed. There was no response when I answered.

Unable to concentrate, I got up and emptied my pockets. Then I noticed something. My cell phone was on, and my home number lit the screen. My cell phone had been calling the home line! I had just made a series of classic "pocket calls."

Several things strike me about this embarrassing episode. Ever since offices have installed multiple lines, people have accidentally called themselves. Yet this was different. I was not even aware of the calls I made. Moreover, a little retrospection highlighted my escalating anger as the calls continued.

I was progressively (and ignorantly) irked by my own actions. I continued to call myself and became increasingly disturbed when someone else was not on the line!

Maybe it is a sign of the times. Our culture seems to worship self-referential thinking. If things are not about us, we tend to check out; and we are often unaware of the way our attitudes and behavior limit engagement with the real world. Legalism smothers the self with outside forces, expectations, and judgments. Antinomianism (the opposite of legalism) not only disregards God's law. While it speaks of direction by the Holy Spirit, it abandons the self to maddening isolation in a hall of mirrors.

Disregard for the Law in Biblical Perspective

The neglect of God's law is full of ironies. The term *antinomianism* is often attributed to Martin Luther, the Protestant reformer who gave animated emphasis to salvation by grace through faith. Some opponents of Luther charged that he disrespected the Law, but Luther actually criticized those who exploited the focus on grace to avoid God's law. Martin Luther may not have believed that people could live the Law wholly, but he did appreciate it as a reminder of our flaws.

Throughout Christian history, those embracing antinomianism have typically claimed that grace offers immediate guidance to replace the Law. This grace is often considered a direct communication from the Holy Spirit. According to the argument, inherited moral norms and descriptions of God's design for behavior are irrelevant.

In one sense, this view appears to be relational. If external moral rules or codes are not the stuff of authentic Christianity, perhaps this notion of intimate Spirit communication is the real deal. However, in practice, antinomianism tends to make claims about the Holy Spirit's presence as a cover for individual whims and desires. There is a glimmer of light in the total disregard for the Law, just as there is a glimmer of light in legalism. Yet the light fades quickly. Antinomianism ends not in relationship with the living God but in the circular prison of self.

Scripture, for all of its amazing emphasis on grace, also condemns the misleading fascination with antinomianism. Paul's confrontation among the church in Corinth may be the most famous example. If anyone preached grace, it was the apostle; but Paul never used grace as a rationale for irresponsible and selfish behavior. He leveled a scathing criticism at one community member engaged in sexual immorality and served notice to the church as a whole (1 Corinthians 5). The writer of Ephesians made a similar point (Ephesians 5). How believers live matters.

Perhaps the most incisive indictment appears among the Pastoral Letters. The author of Second Timothy listed a litany of wrong that would endanger the faithful. Counterfeit teachers would present sinful behavior as nothing more than an interesting way to live. At the top of this list is a term that describes the wayward as "lovers of themselves" (2 Timothy 3:2). There is nothing wrong with a healthy respect for the self; but when everything becomes a matter of self-gratification, we have gone off the rails. Scripture warns that the authentically good news must not be cheapened by this mind-set.

Wesley and the Neglect of God's Law

John Wesley was accused of many things, and some of the accusations had merit. His earliest journey revolved around a fixation on rules and regulations that demonstrated legalism, but the later commitment to holiness rested on grace. Several who claimed that Wesley continued to overstate the importance of works were antinomians. Their dismissal of God's law threatened Wesley's movement as much as any legalism.

Antinomianism in the Methodist movement might be described as too much of a good thing. Wesley was encouraged by Moravian believers during his spiritual crisis of 1738. He found freedom under their insistence that one is saved by faith alone and not through effort. Yet before long Wesley opposed the way his Moravian friends downplayed good works. Wesley's critique continued in his conflict with William Cudworth, a London pastor. Cudworth reasoned that if salvation arrived as a gift of God's righteousness, then good works were unnecessary.

Throughout this debate Wesley was charged with relying on his own righteousness. Those who opposed him professed to depend upon grace. However, Wesley understood the Law as a sign of relationship with God; and he suggested that the antinomian view gave license to selfish behavior. Without God's law, how was one to discern right and wrong? What happened to moral accountability? The mature Wesley did not argue that keeping the Law was a way to earn favor. He did, however, believe that a disregard for the Law was an insult to God.

Readers of John Wesley's theology might arrive at an intriguing insight. The disagreement with antinomian views was not simply a controversy about the Law's role following saving knowledge of Christ. The disagreement revealed conflicting conceptions of the Law itself. Wesley was far more willing to appreciate God's law as a gift. Antinomian positions portrayed the Law as an obligation to be performed through solitary effort.

Yet today some observers conclude that Wesley flirted with legalism, but we might consider a more profound possibility. The antinomians of eighteenth-century England not only invited moral confusion, they also seemed to miss the Law's original intent. This does not mean that a combination of faith and works of the Law can save. Wesley did not teach any such thing. He believed, however, that those saved by grace through faith might receive the Law as a blessing for holy living.

False Freedom

The disregard for God's law in England tended to arise from various kinds of Calvinism. If true Christians are elect and cannot fall from grace, then the Law becomes irrelevant. Taken to an extreme, this view rationalizes that apparently immoral behavior, when expressed by the chosen, is not wrong at all. However, in America the earliest controversies over the law of God followed a different course.

Anne Hutchinson (1591-1643) was a bold Bostonian who taught that the Holy Spirit communicated salvation directly to individuals apart from the Law and apart from the regulations of organized church life. It is not clear that she intended to defend antinomianism, but that is exactly the charge raised against her. Hutchinson's case reminds us that, to a great extent, terms such as *legalism* and *antinomianism* are epithets used against one another. Much that people call legalism is a faithful regard for the moral law, and much that others call antinomianism is a courageous confrontation over worldly power. Anne Hutchinson, no doubt, challenged the earthly rules of male-dominated church authority more than anything else. This does not mean that legalism and antinomianism are imaginary problems. It simply means that such emphases can be exploited through smear tactics.

Perhaps the most controversial expression of American antinomianism took place in Vermont and in Oneida, New York, during the 1830's and 1840's. A restless seer named John Humphrey Noyes gathered many committed to the idea of Christian perfection, but this was perfection of a peculiar sort. These saints understood themselves to be released from established moral norms. Noyes did not quite excuse openly selfish behavior, yet he did develop theories that gave sanction to strange practices. The best known was his belief in "complex marriage." This amounted to approval of shared sexual partners within the religious community.

Asa Mahan's theology of holiness was developed at Oberlin about the time Noyes enjoyed peak notoriety. However, the Oberlin approach was a world removed from that of Noyes; and the difference revolved around God's law. The Oberlin community resembled Wesley, and they distanced themselves from the Oneida group. By Oberlin standards, John Humphrey Noyes was not an authentic student of holiness. He taught "perfectionism," a highly distorted version of the real thing.

The gulf between Oneida and Oberlin was so wide that many accused the Oberlin colony of legalism. The charge is debatable, but it does point to the way Mahan and his colleagues revered God's law. Moreover, this debate regarding the Law unfolded as the writings of a German philosopher were translated into English and contemplated among American colleges. The philosopher was Immanuel Kant, and his thick reasoning affirmed a version of the moral law. Yet Kant's overall viewpoint left a mixed legacy.

Enlightenment?

Immanuel Kant (1724-1804) was one of the most brilliant and detailed thinkers ever known. His tight arguments, awkward writing style, and incessant curiosity about the mind are bewildering. I remember reading Kant as a college student, sitting in a residence hall basement with an English translation of the philosopher and a dictionary. Where did he find such words? What did they mean? Kant is easy to dismiss because he is so hard to understand, but a little patience is important here. He had a profound effect on the course of Western thought, and his work should not be tossed out simply because it is dense. Today's cultural assumptions about what we can and cannot know for sure owe much to Immanuel Kant.

Kant, like many philosophers, wanted bedrock upon which to rest knowledge. During his studies he developed a doubt regarding our ability to know the world around us.

Sure, we live as if we know the people and things encountered in daily life; but how do we know that what we encounter is real? Kant's thought led him to place less emphasis on the certainty of objective knowledge and more emphasis on the knowing subject. Maybe knowledge has more to do with our categories of perception than the stuff that is supposedly "out there." It may not be a correct approach to the universe, but it is also not quite as outlandish as it sounds. After all, there are many things we presume to know that seem different when viewed from another perspective. Some objects baffle us entirely. Perhaps there are things we will never know.

Kant was a representative of the eighteenth-century Enlightenment, a movement that sought to open new understandings of the mind and world without resorting to religious authority. Not all Enlightenment thinkers attacked religion, and some used their philosophy to support traditional beliefs. Not all took Immanuel Kant's approach, either. In fact, some did just the opposite. Instead of relying on categories of reasoning, many trusted experience. In recent years it has become fashionable to blame the Enlightenment for most of our contemporary problems, but this is an oversimplification. There were good and perhaps not so good qualities among this intellectual movement.

To his credit, Immanuel Kant sought a clear understanding of the moral law. He is the philosopher who gave us the "categorical imperative," a principle that defended people as ends in themselves.[1] However, Kant's theory of knowledge got in the way of his moral conviction. Because he suspected that we may be incapable of knowing the external world, he would not ground his ethics in knowledge of others. Kant's morality was more about the acting subject than the value of those around us.

The German philosopher even said that any reliance on knowledge of others for ethical guidance constituted heteronomy, that manipulative dynamic of controlling rules. The only way to avoid heteronomy was through a moral law that remained true to the self. This law Kant termed *autonomy* (from the Greek *autos*, meaning "self," and *nomos*, meaning "law").

Today many indict autonomy as an individualism that ends in selfishness. Immanuel Kant did not intend for it to be anything other than a sound principle of morality. Perhaps a law rooted in our nature is the best guide. There is some credibility to his claim, but there is also a nagging question. Can a law so identified with the self help us respect others? Kant's moral theory reflected the alienation he perceived between us and the world around us.

Antinomianism and autonomy are not the same, but they share certain characteristics. The disregard for God's law (antinomianism) may believe in Spirit guidance that surpasses the Law. Yet it inevitably gets tangled in self-interest and capricious behavior. Moral principle that comes from the self (autonomy) may hope to treat others as ends in themselves, yet it cannot know others and their intrinsic worth. Both antinomianism and autonomy leave us isolated and fail to help us get over ourselves.

The Intellectual's New Clothes

One problem with perspectives that celebrate the self is their apparent superiority over religious tradition. Release from rules, regulations, and other burdens outside the self may be genuine freedom; and believers who throw off exterior demands and worn-out expectations may experience grace. After all, such liberation typically includes an awareness of the self as inherently valuable.

There is much to admire in a positive sense of self, and authentic grace challenges the burdens placed upon us by human powers. However, there can also be a confusion of relationships in the focus upon self. It is one thing to know release from legalistic burdens; it is another thing to experience grace as a gift from God. The two can be one and the same, but the first is not necessarily the second.

Once believers go down the road of self-admiration, it is difficult to offer them anything more. I have known congregations that were tremendously legalistic about traditions and certain formulations of doctrine. I have also known congregations that claimed to move beyond backward thinking. These churches had their own distinctive culture. For one, they chased intellectual fads and typically spoke of themselves as advanced Christians. They never lacked the confidence to consider themselves at least a little more astute than the average body of believers.

Scholars have suggested that there are stages of faith, that people progress from one worldview to another. The movement beyond legalism to a higher regard for the self is often described in such theories. It is not at all a bad thing when placed within the whole sweep of grace and the journey of faith. However, this movement is not the destination many envision. Faith includes freedom from excessive obligation, but it is much more than self-regard. Sadly, many who claim to be liberated have simply thrown off tradition without embracing any meaningful alternative. There is little worse than driving with abandon down a road, only to discover that it is a dead end.

Colleges and universities are notorious environments for expatriate Christians, sophisticated people who have left simplistic backgrounds. Too often, however, many confuse an exodus from legalism with something more promising. It may take intellectual fortitude to leave oppressive religious backgrounds, but simply walking away does not make for a deep life.

Those in the church who bemoan the way our academic institutions have abandoned the faith often get it wrong. Thinking people are not the problem. However, people who think that criticism of established beliefs is enough do fall short. There is something beyond the tearing down of old thought-structures, but we need the insight and the courage to step out and beyond our self-proclaimed genius.

An embrace of relationship with God is forward motion, not a retreat to easy answers.

Identity Implosion

The practical effect of much "enlightened" thinking is narcissism, a distorted love of the self. Narcissus, remember, was the character who fell in love with his own reflection. Sound familiar? The examples from our culture are so numerous that it hardly seems helpful to list them. We have had plenty of theological exploration already regarding our society's superficial focus on the self, and many of these observations are right. The worship of celebrities, sports personalities, and CEOs (who, in turn, worship themselves) is but one expression of the sickness. My aim is not to rail at these tempting targets. Rather, I suggest that the pervasive attitude is nourished by intellectual assumptions. Our culture may not invoke particular philosophies when expressing and justifying self-centered behaviors, but certain legacies of thinking are at play.

Moreover, it is easy to identify narcissism in others. Confronting it within ourselves is difficult. I can always find evidence of someone else's self-absorption, especially when it threatens me! Legalism is not the only way we compete with one another. In a world of isolated selves, anything and anyone who dares to question my supremacy must go. There is a desperate quality to this competitive existence. Winning is not enough. We must win in ever bigger proportion just to preserve the self. Even then there is a haunting, perhaps subconscious, insecurity that the life of isolated striving is not real.

Some years ago, writer Paul Ricoeur offered a provocative suggestion.[2] Ricoeur posited that intellectual growth might follow a three-fold pattern. First, according to Ricoeur, we accept the world as given. We inherit belief systems, ways of viewing things, and certain religious convictions. Second, perhaps, we test these inherited norms and perspectives.

We may leave them entirely for a while or for good. Yet some move beyond simplistic acceptance and critical rejection to a third posture. This Ricoeur called a "second naiveté." His choice of language is at once intriguing and troubling. Few of us want to be naive; and many consider our earliest, simplest understandings to be just that. Many will grow beyond rigid beliefs, and many will also declare that the move beyond our first beliefs is genuine maturity.

However, Ricoeur challenges us to consider that there is a kind of second naiveté beyond our first understandings and our criticisms. This second naiveté involves giving ourselves to something or someone. Those who move ahead cannot remain isolated from others and wrapped up in self-assured critique of the world.

This third movement is dangerous. It can be used as an excuse to accept bondage once again. People often give themselves over to the same oppressive dynamics that held them long before. Yet this third movement holds promise. It can represent a brand-new giving of the self to God and others.

There is an irony here, too. Our search for the self in isolation from the outside world is doomed. Only in relationship do we find our identity. This does not mean that we discover ourselves through controlling relationships. Rather, we discover ourselves through relationship with the living God. Additionally, this is not something we invent or determine. God entered the world and gave to us before we ever considered giving our lives to God.

So despite our understandable fear of being measured against others, there is something about us that remains unknown until illumined by an external reality. That reality is God. We are not created and set adrift. We are called into being and kept alive by holy conversation, and the voice that gives us identity comes from God. This divine address can be confused with worldly noise, but it cannot be replaced. There are plenty of competing voices out there, and they are all happy to tell us who we are. However, only God has the power to reveal our real selves.

Some years after writing his book on holiness, Asa Mahan moved to Michigan and founded Adrian College. By then he was a veteran educator and an antislavery/ women's rights activist. He was also a bit of an absent-minded professor. The students were especially fond of Mahan and called him The Old Doctor. His flowing beard, booming voice, and spiritual energy made him a lovably eccentric person. The only complaint raised against Mahan by students related to his illegible handwriting. It was said that reading the Greek language was easy when compared to deciphering his notes.

A story has been handed down about one time Mahan stepped into the Adrian post office to retrieve his mail. In those days citizens simply approached the service counter, gave their name, and waited for a clerk to bring the mail forward. One day Mahan walked into the establishment while deep in thought. Distracted and lost in contemplation, he failed to notice a new clerk at the window. Mahan was jolted from his meditation when the man asked, "What name?" Startled and confused, the college president could not compose himself in order to reply. He stared at the clerk, but no words came out. After an extremely awkward moment he turned and began to leave. On his way out he was greeted by an old friend: "How do you do, Dr. Mahan?" The president wheeled around and proclaimed, "That's it!" He returned to the counter, gave his name, and received the mail.[3]

This piece of lore may stretch the facts, but it does illustrate a point. There is something about all of us that remains unknown until named by someone else. Friends can help with this process, but only God can tell us who we are. Living the way of holiness is not an exercise in isolation. It is, at its essence, an expression of relationship. Holiness embodies a perpetual dialogue with God. By knowing God, we come to know ourselves. We also come to know and love others.

---

1. From *Groundwork of the Metaphysic of Morals*, by Immanuel Kant, translated and analyzed by H. J. Paton (Harper & Row, 1964); page 96.
2. From *The Symbolism of Evil*, by Paul Ricoeur, translated from the French by Emerson Buchanan (Beacon Press, 1967); page 352.
3. From "A Pioneer College President," in *The Methodist Recorder*, by D. S. Stephens (September 11, 1926); page 7.

CHAPTER FOUR

When Freedom Means Relationship

"And all of us, with unveiled faces, seeing the glory of the Lord as though reflected in a mirror, are being transformed into the same image from one degree of glory to another; for this comes from the Lord, the Spirit."
—2 Corinthians 3:18

Laura Smith Haviland was in trouble. Unpretentious and overburdened, she needed help. During the 1830's, she and her husband, Charles, settled in the wilderness of Michigan and began to raise a family. They initiated anti-slavery and humanitarian projects; but in 1845, an epidemic swept the countryside. Charles died, as did their twenty-two-month-old daughter, along with both of Laura's parents. She almost fell to the disease but recovered.

Haviland was thirty-six years old, widowed, living on a small farm, with several remaining children under her care. She was also in debt, and her creditors would not adjust any obligations. The men who held notes against her insisted that she pay, and most of them expressed the arrogant and insulting view that a woman could not manage such a situation. She was in trouble.

Years later Haviland recalled a dream that came to her during this turmoil. The vision of an angelic host opened around her. One of the beings took Haviland's hand, and she felt confident enough to ask for a name. "My name is Supporter," the angel replied. Haviland asked about another figure and received an answer: "Her name is Influencer-of-Hearts." A third angel was named "Searcher-of-Hearts." Haviland realized that the names of each angel revealed a divine mission. One of the beings said to Supporter, "Support her, for she needs it." The angel by that name reached for Haviland's other hand. With both of her hands in the comforting grip of this guardian, a wave of strength passed over her and filled her soul. She was not alone. Her troubles remained, but she woke with a sense of peace: "Calm and sweet was this confidence in being cared for, and supported by an almighty arm."[1]

Today, Haviland is remembered as a fearless leader on the Underground Railroad, a woman who ran an integrated school for young people, a prophetic worker against alcohol abuse, and an advocate for women's rights. Her life of service is explored in history books and revered by many. During the Civil War she traveled to places of devastation and offered relief through food, clothing, and medical care. She challenged generals and civilian administrators to do more about appalling conditions. She was a tough character, and she did not take guff from anyone.

Haviland not only managed to cope with the immediate crises of her earlier years, she helped a nation cope with astounding pain and brokenness; and she did it with grit and grace. All of humanity knew no better friend. Few (if any) remember Haviland as a timid person. She embodied a strength that remains rare, but she could do so because of her reliance on God.

What is it about authentically strong people that points to God? Our culture makes the idea of strength an idol; but this is a counterfeit strength, a brittle strength that breaks under pressure. Real strength is something else, something more. It is a willingness to trust God and move forward. The Laura Havilands among us are not impressed with societal power. They understand their resources as divine gifts. However, such witnesses demonstrate a resilient, persistent, wide-reaching impact precisely because they are sustained by the almighty God. A need for God is no weakness; it is the very secret of poise and authority.

Command and Promise

Holiness is not a matter of individual achievement. Thinking it is so has been a serious problem. There are many implications to such an assumption. For one, it invites failure. If I stand before God with nothing more than my solitary competence, I am on thin ice. Moreover, a trust in individual ability inevitably leads to exhaustion. The stress of trying again and again to pull oneself up by the moral bootstraps is grueling. Most of us want to live well—do right—participate in the good; but aiming for this ideal can wear us down. I will only speak for myself. When I am burned out, beat up, and dispirited, I am not likely to live the way of holiness.

Perhaps that is why John Wesley's exploration of Matthew 5:17 arrives as liberation. Jesus said, " 'Do not think that I have come to abolish the law or the prophets; I have come not to abolish but to fulfill.' " Over the years this verse has received varied treatments, and some interpretations have minimized the Law's lasting significance. According to this view, Jesus fulfilled the Law in his life, death, and resurrection so that it no longer has authority for Christians. John Wesley did not buy such thinking. He claimed that Jesus fulfilled the Law in a way that makes it even more relevant. Yet this does not mean that the Law is, by nature, a burden. On the contrary, it indicates a terrific gift.

Wesley believed that the Law reveals a command and a promise. In other words, he suggested that any expectation within the Law is rendered possible by grace. Believers often underrate their ability to live God's way because they try to do so alone. Wesley wrote:

43

There is no need for the law to pass away, in order to the establishing of the gospel. Indeed neither of them supersedes the other, but they agree perfectly well together. Yea, the very same words, considered in different respects, are parts both of the law and of the gospel. If they are considered as commandments, they are parts of the law: if as promises, of the gospel. Thus, 'Thou shalt love the Lord thy God with all thy heart,' when considered as a commandment, is a branch of the law; when regarded as a promise, is an essential part of the gospel—the gospel being no other than the commands of the law proposed by way of promises.[2]

Wesley's carefully woven language should give us pause. His words read as though law and gospel complete one another. This may make some nervous. Did John Wesley fall back into legalism here? I don't think so.

While we have never been able to shake our legalistic inclinations, it is advantageous to appear as defenders of grace. When Wesley suggested that command and promise belong together, we may object that this is an unreasonable expectation; but do we let go of controlling behavior? Charges of legalism can be devices to avoid responsibility. They can also be ways to assert power over others. Those who appoint themselves protectors of grace enjoy a presumed moral superiority. A better approach would simply ponder Wesley's expression.

John Wesley's interpretation demonstrates his realization that the Law was designed as a way and not a weapon. Behind this insight stood a fundamental conviction regarding the being and attributes of God. Wesley knew a God of unlimited authority and inexhaustible love. If the mighty God called for particular action, then this same God possessed the resources to sustain such a life. Perhaps all would not grasp the connection and receive the gift of guidance, but there was no theological reason for anticipating less.

Wesley did have high expectations, but they were expectations of God. We might call it trust or even faith. God may not grant us every request. There are certainly times when life presents excruciating experiences that are not relieved. Yet when it comes to living the way intended for us, God can be counted on to deliver.

The Evangelical Spirit

Wesley's perspective is an example of that which Asa Mahan came to call the evangelical spirit. Today, the word *evangelical* has been embraced or discarded because of its identification with a particular cultural movement. This is a shame. The word, in its origins, celebrates God's good news of grace. Authentic evangelicalism does not require agreement with doctrinal minutia or predetermined political views. It acknowledges that we are saved and empowered by grace.

This is what Mahan meant when he said that the evangelical spirit offers a way beyond legalism and antinomianism. Legalism seeks to earn God's love and uses the law to control others. Antinomianism runs away from God's law in the name of grace. The evangelical spirit trusts that God can redeem and restore. God can save us from our self-deceiving desires to manipulate the Law, and God can save us from our self-defeating neglect of the Law.

Once again twentieth-century theologian Paul Tillich offers intriguing parallels. Tillich suggested that legalism might be described as heteronomy, the heavy and controlling demands that come from outside of us. While not precisely the same thing, antinomianism resembles autonomy, that captivity to the self. Tillich suggested that beyond heteronomy and autonomy there is a third way. This he termed theonomy (from the Greek *theos*, meaning "God," and *nomos*, meaning "law"). Simply put, the word describes God's law; but its simplicity has sometimes been misrepresented.

45

Theonomy is not a series of codes and rules that should be passed into civil law. Some assume that this is exactly the meaning of the term, but they are mistaken. Turning all kinds of religious codes into civil law is theocracy, not theonomy. Real theonomy describes the law God wants to write on our hearts. Wesley may not have used the language, but he had something much like theonomy in mind when he argued that God's command to love is also a promise.

Promises are the stuff of relationships. They come from beyond us, but they do not come as burdens. If the evangelical spirit is about anything, it is about a living relationship that sustains us. This same relationship also empowers us to love others. A favorite text of holiness writers has been 2 Corinthians 3:18: "And all of us, with unveiled faces, seeing the glory of the Lord as though reflected in a mirror, are being transformed into the same image from one degree of glory to another; for this comes from the Lord, the Spirit." The complex structure of this passage makes it enticing and somewhat difficult to translate.

We might notice that God's face is not described as unveiled. Our faces are unveiled here. Our open faces see God's glory reflected in something or someone. The New International Version translates the verse to say that we reflect God's glory. This is a valid reading of the end result; but, first, we behold or see God's glory. We meet the glory of God in the face of Jesus Christ (2 Corinthians 4:6). Then we reflect God's glory among others.

Any glory communicated by us is reflected glory. It is glory that originates with God and then is communicated to us through Christ. As we receive such glory, we are transformed into the image of Christ, "who is the image of God" (2 Corinthians 4:4). The process of transformation leads us to reflect God's love toward others.

Two truths are named in this text. First, we are not the origin of light; God is. Second, we cannot keep the light; it must be reflected beyond us to others. Considered more positively, the text captures the command to pass God's love on and the promise that we may receive this power from the very source of love.

As They Are

The relational view of holiness expressed by 2 Corinthians 3 is also grounded in certain philosophical convictions. Not all modern philosophies have gone down the road charted by Immanuel Kant. Some approaches accept that we may know the world around us with at least a degree of certainty. This view does not pretend to know everything. It simply moves beyond the conclusion that we are doomed entirely to subjective perceptions. Philosophers call this realism because it holds that despite our limitations, we do know significant aspects of reality. For instance, we can know God; and we can get over ourselves long enough to know others.

There is a telling passage in a book on philosophy written by Asa Mahan. When critiquing Immanuel Kant, the holiness professor remarked that we may indeed know the world around us. In fact, Mahan believed that we can see "with open face realities as they are."[3] This emphasis on seeing with open faces resembles the language of 2 Corinthians 3:18. Mahan the holiness advocate was also Mahan the realist philosopher. He knew God through Jesus Christ and knew and loved others. He did not obsess over his personal perceptions. He got outside of himself.

Maybe more than anything else, today's holiness movement needs to focus on the world outside. Intentions and purity of heart are important, but seeing those our culture ignores is absolutely critical. Modern subjectivism may seem like an honorably modest way to approach the world. If I am not sure that my perceptions are conclusive, then I must moderate my claims. I may even be moved to acknowledge the views of others. Such humility is good, but subjectivism is rarely so humble.

When we shift from the world around us to our perceptions of reality, we also open the door for self-interested
behavior. If things (and perhaps people) are not necessarily
as they seem, then why should I take them seriously? If my
perception is what matters, then why worry about much
else? We may not adopt this reasoning on purpose, but it
inevitably leaks into our assumptions.

Modern subjectivism often claims that it is open-minded
when it is something else entirely. Realism might seem to be
overconfident about knowing the world around us. Yet it
also takes that world (and other people) seriously. An hon-
est realism forces us to deal with the truth outside.

Why is it, then, that so many people are simply written
off by our culture? If one does not represent the "right" cor-
ner of the world; the "right" socioeconomic background;
the "right" color, gender, or race, one is invisible. This is
wrong, and those committed to holiness can offer a correc-
tive vision. Love is so much more than feelings. It is the
recognition and honoring of value. It may travel through
my heart, but it does not originate there. Love is God's great
initiative. We are privileged to participate in a miracle of
affirmation.

Free to Love

John Wesley's notion of command and promise makes
living the Law a matter of grace. However, the Law itself is
a gift. Many may think of God's law as a detailed bundle of
expectations that can wear us down, but what if the moral
law is actually about intrinsic worth? All would be valued
as they are, and that includes us. People often behave in
ways that are hard to appreciate, and we must separate
actions from essential value. Yet living the Law as a regard
for God-established worth allows us to share grace, and
there is no greater blessing than being an ambassador of
God's grace.

Moreover, the life of holiness offers great freedom. When we affirm the intrinsic value of people, we acknowledge God's authority. We accept God's determination of worth. I am not in charge of measuring value. I may act as if I would like this job, but it is a terrible task. Whenever I try to usurp God in this role, I make a mess of things. This does not mean that I am obligated to support all that people do. Grace is an affirmation of being, not behavior.

This also does not mean that I am obligated to live the agendas of others. A life of holiness will direct our hearts beyond the self, but at the same time we must be intentional about how we give those hearts away. Anyone seriously concerned for others will encounter people who desire to control the expression of that concern. Giving ourselves to scripted programs, even if they represent legitimate movements, is not necessarily ministry; and it is certainly not freedom. In fact, it may be a kind of aimlessness that serves controlling personalities; and that sounds more like heteronomy to me.

We are responsible for discovering how God would like for us to give ourselves away. If we have understood the moral law with some clarity, then our holy living will affirm the intrinsic worth of others. However, it must also affirm our intrinsic worth. Allowing ourselves to be used by aggressive people or organizations is not healthy. Giving ourselves to those who lack power is an affirmation of the self and others.

Finding your particular expression of holiness is an adventure of some mystery. There are books on discovering one's purpose, and many of them are quite good. Yet holiness is not about following proven methods for unlocking the secrets of life. I have become convinced that my vocation or calling includes making a case for the intrinsic worth of all people. Sure, this is a theoretical notion; and it may seem like something that none would contest. However, our culture does not operate as if all matter; and I hear God through my discontent and wondering about the issue.

Your call may be different; and it takes listening, as well. That is why this could never be a spiritual "how-to" book. As much as I might want to make it such a thing, it cannot be done. We can consider theological meanings and stories that inspire, but ultimately we live personal narratives in conversation with God.

Sanctified Common Sense

Near the end of her long life, Laura Haviland wrote, "Is it not the duty of every Christian to bring his or her religion into every line of life-work, and act as conscientiously in politics as in church work? Sanctified common sense is loudly called for on the highway of holiness."[4] She made this statement as a response to the social problems of her day—especially the addiction to alcohol, the abuse of women, and the exploitation of children.

It is no accident that Haviland referred to conscientious political involvement as sanctified common sense. The Wesleyan emphasis on holiness is intensely personal, a matter of relationship with God through Jesus Christ. However, it is also social. Intimacy with God will change us and move us to change things for the better. That is all part of reflecting God's image.

This does not mean that God sanctifies every political initiative, and Haviland's intriguing terminology is a subtle guide for us. Sanctified common sense may seem like a description of ordinary thinking that serves a religious purpose. Yet there was a day when *common sense* referred to an intentional philosophy of life. This perspective featured the intellectual and moral interests shared by humanity. Common sense pointed to the common good and the value of all. It was a term associated with the philosophy of realism, too. What might sanctified common sense look like today?

Principled social action and political advocacy respect the intrinsic worth and participation of all. This sensitivity is not as abstract as it may sound. Much that masquerades as Christian social concern today is a defense of self-interest and privilege. Part of giving our lives away to Christ should include public concern for those without voice and power. A sense that is common will travel Haviland's "highway of holiness."

This road is demanding and liberating, and the journey will not automatically support any one political party. Quite frankly, none of the major parties in America represent the values of holiness. Some capture aspects of sanctified common sense, but they do so imperfectly. We need to be careful before giving ourselves to political agendas. Giving oneself entirely to God in Christ is not the same thing as choosing a party platform.

However, the way of holiness will call us to get involved from the standpoint of God-established values. We may feel like odd characters at times, unable to endorse the powerful machinery of party mobilization; but we can make a difference in the political process through our unique witness. Note the fatigue of people during election season. Many want something more from their public involvement, something higher, something inspired. The tradition of holy love has much to offer. It does not tell people how to vote, but it provides deep and abiding principles that can cut through the noise of most campaigns.

Your Story

We need real holiness today more than ever. Consider one issue: slavery. John Wesley distinguished himself in many ways, but the uncompromising opposition to slavery remains one of his most prophetic legacies. His 1774 "Thoughts Upon Slavery" leveled a withering indictment against this demonic institution. A few days before he died, Wesley sent a letter of encouragement to William Wilberforce, the person typically remembered as England's premier abolitionist. He noted the almost overwhelming challenge but insisted that

" 'if God be for you, who can be against you?' "[5] God's call to love and justice is always accompanied by God's grace and empowerment.

Early American holiness advocates also led the fight against slavery. Imagine their exhilaration when, during 1865, the United States embraced the Thirteenth Amendment to the Constitution and made slavery a national crime. For generations we have looked back on this horrible practice as a sad chapter in history; but we have also assumed that the matter is settled, that it has been relegated to the past. This is not so.

Today it is estimated that twenty-seven million people are held in slavery throughout the world. This contemporary slavery is often called human trafficking because its victims are bought and sold and moved from one place to another like merchandise. Documented forms of such slavery vary. Many instances fall within a worldwide system of sexual exploitation. Other expressions reveal a proliferation of bonded labor. Among areas torn by war, children are often considered property and forced to serve in violent militia groups.

The United States is not above the problem. Cases of slavery have been exposed in a variety of American enterprises —from the restaurant, hotel/motel, and agricultural industries to individualized arrangements of domestic help. According to the US government, somewhere between 14,500 and 17,500 people are trafficked into the United States each year. Roughly eighty percent of the trafficking victims are female, and seventy percent of female victims are pressed into the commercial sex trade. I know friends who have offered shelter for victims seeking to escape powerful and brutal traffickers. It is the Underground Railroad all over again.

We need real holiness today more than ever. The God-established intrinsic worth of people remains under siege. Now it is time for you to write your story. How will you receive the unconditional love of God in Christ and make a difference? Do not let others suggest that you cannot be a person of holiness. All you need to do is say yes to God's love and yes to the value of others.

---

1. From *A Woman's Life Work*, by Laura Haviland (S. B. Shaw, 1902); pages 48-49.
2. From *The Works of John Wesley*, Volume 1, edited by Albert C. Outler (Abingdon Press, 1984); page 554.
3. From *The Science of Natural Theology,* by Asa Mahan (Henry Hoyt, 1867); page 62.
4. From *A Woman's Life Work*; page 566.
5. From *The Works of John Wesley*, Volume XIII; page 153.

For Reflection and Discussion

Chapter One

1. When you think of holiness in the Old Testament, what comes to mind?

2. What are the similarities and differences between Old Testament and New Testament expressions of holiness?

3. How would you describe John Wesley's understanding of holiness following his Aldersgate experience?

4. How did Asa Mahan define *love*?

5. How does the cross of Jesus affirm the worth of people?

6. How does the resurrection of Jesus affirm the worth of people?

Chapter Two

1. How do legalism and antinomianism leave us with little more than our own resources?

2. What was the attitude of Jesus toward God's law?

3. How did John Wesley understand the "third use" of the Law?

4. How does God's law become something other than an authentic gift?

5. Why do you think our culture tends to calculate worth according to performance?

Chapter Three

1. How might the Protestant focus on salvation by grace through faith invite neglect of God's law?

2. How did John Wesley encounter a neglect of the Law, and how did he respond to the challenge?

3. How did antinomianism express itself in early American church life, and what were the consequences of this view?

4. What is autonomy, and how can it lead to isolation from one another?

5. What problems do we experience when trying to understand ourselves apart from a relationship with God?

Chapter Four

1. What did John Wesley mean when he connected *command* and *promise*?

2. What did Asa Mahan intend to describe when he spoke of an evangelical spirit?